Crimson Letters

Stanzas from the Heart

Shantanu Paul

Made with ❤ on the BookLeaf Publishing Platform
www.bookleafpub.in
www.bookleafpub.com

Dedication

To the timeless whispers of the muse and the relentless spirits that dare to dream and feel, this collection is dedicated. May these verses serve as a mirror to your innermost thoughts and a window to vistas yet explored. Here's to the seekers of beauty in the cacophony of existence; may you find peace in these words.

Preface

In the quiet corridors of the human heart, where words
often tread softly, poetry finds its sacred echo. This
collection is an ode to the myriad expressions that paint
our shared experiences with strokes both delicate and
daring. Each poem herein is a whisper, a shout, a tear,
and a laugh shared between the lines of our unspoken
realities.

We traverse through gardens of blooming metaphors
under the nurturing sunlight of introspection, and we
walk the dimly lit alleys of our fears, guided only by the
gentle lantern of carefully chosen words. These verses
are mirrors held up to the soul of the world, reflecting its
complex beauty, its raw pain, and its unyielding hope.

Crafted with reverence for the timeless art that connects
us all, these poems aspire not merely to be read, but to
be lived. Through them, may you journey deep within
and far beyond, finding traces of yourself in the
silhouette of every stanza.

Embark on this lyrical voyage, where language dances
and emotions transcend, and where every page turned is
a new horizon. Here's to finding infinity within the finite

and discovering that within poetry lies the profound power to both question and quiet, to unsettle and to uplift.

Welcome, dear reader, to a sanctuary of syllables that both echo and await your own voice's resonance.

Acknowledgements

In the weaving of these verses, a multitude of threads have entwined, bearing the colors of many souls. To those luminaries who illuminated the dark recesses of my thoughts—my fervent gratitude.

To my family, whose enduring support cradles my every word; you are both the harbor and the sea from which my expressions sail forth.

To my mentors, who have polished the lens through which I view the world, transforming rough glass into the spectacles of clarity—thank you for teaching me to see.

To my friends, whose laughter and critiques have been the anvil and hammer shaping the form of my creations —you are the alchemists of my joy and resolve.

To the past poets, who converse with me across the chasms of time and space through their indelible marks on pages yellowed and worn—I am eternally in your debt.

To the silence of early mornings, which has cradled the

seeds of tumultuous thoughts until they burst into bloom
—I owe the tranquillity that fosters creation.

And to you, the unseen muses who visit me in the
rustling leaves, the whisper of the wind, the bustling city
streets, and the quiet moments of solitude—thank you for
filling the well from which I draw inspiration.

Each poem within this collection owes its life not just to
me but to all who have touched my life. You are all a part
of this tapestry, subtly woven into the very fibers of my
being. For your presence, support, and love, I am
endlessly grateful.

1. Finding Solace in Wild Embrace

Amidst the shadows of my mounting dread,
As silence breaks by whispers in the dark,
When thoughts of future fears through my mind tread,
To nature's arms I flee, where solace marks.

There, by the lake, where quiet reeds sway,
The solitary heron hunts with grace,
Unburdened by the woes of coming days,
In tranquil waters finds its rightful place.

The wilderness, a refuge for my soul,
Hosts creatures clad in calm and simple might,
No burden of tomorrow takes its toll,
They rest in moments, far from human plight.

Beneath the canopy where stars shy hide,
Their gentle glow a balm for weary eyes,
In this embrace of earth I dare confide,
Released from worldly binds, my spirit flies.

For here, amidst the whispers of the trees,
Enveloped in the dance of life and light,
I find a strength bestowed by gentle breeze,
Within the grace of nature, I alight.

2. The Inevitability of Purpose

In every soul, a secret point of gravity,
Hidden or veiled;
A purpose within, holding its own veracity,
Always hailed.

Confessed in whispers by our inward voice, so light,
Perhaps too pure,
For the bold claims of day's assertive light,
To endure.

Held in reverence, as delicate as lace,
To grasp,
Might seem as futile as tracing echoes in space,
Or a clasp.

Yet, we trace it still, firmer for the miles we tread;
Lofty dreams,
Like the steady climb of mountains overhead,
In moonbeams.

Possibly untouched by the trials of day,
However,
Infinity gives us courage to sway,
Forever.

Each attempt, a testament to our spirit's fire,
Ignites anew,
With celestial resilience, never to tire,
Always true.

3. The Known Unknown

The moment arose, indeed,
When staying closed, a dire need,
Became a burden too grave to bear,
Than the unfolding into open air.

For to bloom required daring,
Yet in growth, there's no comparing
To the suffocation of unspent grace,
Than to flourish in the light's embrace.

Thus, from the safety of the known,
Into the vast unknown, thrown;
To brave the elements in full array,
For the promise of the light of day.

What once was fear of outward show,
Now a fearless need to grow,
For the agony of tight-clenched dreams
Is greater than it once had seemed.

4. Symphony of My True Essence

In the veins of my essence, truths deeply thread,
No falsehoods here; in my flesh, they've not spread.
Believe me, this knowledge, it roots in my core,
Pure and resolute, and longing to soar.

History's weight nests within every cell,
Suggesting no substitute, no parallel shell.
Though minor my woes may seem from outside,
Within these bones, my own stories reside.

They groan, they protest, signaling strife,
Announcing that they, alone, animate life.
This skeletal framework, uniquely my own,
Echoes each joy, every ache I've known.

To forsake, to neglect what in sinews does run,
Is to deny the battles my body has won.
So hear me and know this, in marrow and spine,
The pulse that propels me is singularly mine.

5. Folly of Haste

What are our days, if bound in haste,
Devoid of moments to taste the air?

No pause to lie beneath the trees,
Nor watch the dancing leaves and breeze.

No chance to notice, on our walk,
The intricate spider's web or hawk.

No moments spared in light of day,
To see the river's sparkle play.

No leisure to observe the grace
Of moonlight on the night's embrace.

No breaks to hear the silent cues
When morning dew embraces hues.

Such empty lives we lead with dread,
If never we breathe, but rush instead.

6. The Unconfined within the Confines

In the confines of my own existence refined,
My days stretched just as far as they were confined.
Its spirit matched the breadth of spirit's space,
With life's machinery purring in its commonplace.

Above, the grand ballet of celestial grace,
Underneath, nature's whispers filled the base.
Journeys spanned the heights and the depths, traced
By silent hooves, wings, and dreams unchased.

Adorned in the ordinary - socks, and hats, and skin,
Nourished by the rituals of daily bread and tin.
It closed and opened—fingers and panes,
In its simplicity, profound thoughts remain.

Some lives sprawl wider, others shrink to terse,
And the weight of living varies universe to universe.
Together we laughed; together kneaded dough,
Shared the subtleties that only close quarters know.

Then a phase of estrangement, a wanting retreat,
A week apart; thoughts of others fleet.
But hunger returned me to my essential feast,
Where my life and I, cloaked in our need, unleashed.

In mutual craving, our essence interlaced,
With voracity for living that couldn't be erased.
Through the weave and weft of our beings combined,
We found the vast within, the unconfined.

7. The Essence of Now

Bask in the now, seize the sublime sight
Savor each second of day and the night
Notice the world, every detail, and sound
Here in this instant where life is found

Wander not into the future unseen
Embrace the present, where life convenes
Treasure this time, offer your zest
In these brief moments, give nothing but best

Let not tomorrow your now undermine
Or countless moments might fleetingly decline
With those beside you, in shared time so dear
Focus with fervor, let distractions veer

Laugh till the echoes fill up the air,
Let sorrow's tears fall, show that you care
Pack each minute with fervor and zeal
Open to teachings each moment can reveal

Alert and eager, let complacency fade
For in a flicker, life's alterations are made
Each tick is potent, with potential so vast
Once it has vanished, it joins the past

Sixty small seconds, a minuscule frame
Might forge connections, love proclaim
Or witness beginnings, see journeys' ends
In these tiny fragments, your path wends

You're sculpted by seconds, by minutes made
Not by the taking, but love that's conveyed
Live through each moment, embrace the true worth
For each fleeting instant gives birth to your earth

Life's but an album of moments so rare
Each one a treasure that's yours to care
Waste not the riches that time imparts
The value of life is the sum of its parts.

8. The Grand Performance

What is this existence? A stage of fervor,
Our laughter echoes through the halls of discord,
Within our mothers' depths, we're clothed for the show,
A fleeting act beneath the cosmos' glow.
The heavens watch, keen eyes that rarely miss,
Observing each misstep in our earthly script.
Our final beds obscure us from the day,
As curtains close when actors fade away.
Thus we proceed, in roles until the end,
Our final breath, a truth we can't pretend.

9. Engaged Disengaged

Engaged am I, yet not as many conceive,
In realms unseen where thoughts and dreams weave.
Engaged in quelling the terrors untold,
In seeking the brave within me, bold.

Engaged with the voices small yet profound,
In little whispers, life's truths are found.
Engaged in embracing the tangible grace
Of nature's quiet, a grounding embrace.

Engaged in the nurture of root and of bloom,
In touching the earth, finding peace in its loom.
Engaged in the art of challenging thought,
Refining my views, untangling the fraught.

Engaged wholly in the dance of the now,
In moments fleeting, to life, I vow.
Not busy as the world defines this chase,
But filled with living—not merely a race.

10. A Raven's Whisper

In the quiet hush,
A raven's brush
Cast flakes of frost
From the pine, wind-tossed.

It stirred my soul,
A subtle shift,
And gently stole
The clouds that drift.

A lightness borne,
From shadows' sway,
This moment torn
From a darker day.

11. Unshackling From Shadows

Yesterdays linger in shadows cast,
Reserved for a realm where they're meant to last,
Yet some spirits hold tight to this spectral hand,
As it carves its despair in the grains of sand.

Fixated they stay on the echoes of self,
On chapters closed, on a dusty shelf,
Grasping at ghosts of missteps gone by,
Blind to the truth no tear can deny.

For the dance of time is a forward flow,
No step retraced, no backward toe,
Try as you might with all your might,
The past is a script in perpetual night.

What unfolds each day is a mystery dress,
Woven with strands of aimless guess,
Embrace the cards dealt by fate's own hand,
Reveal your plot, let your tale expand.

Shed the cloak of yesterday's gloom,
Bask in today's invigorating bloom,
For now is the breath of a new endeavor,
The moment to seize and cherish forever.

Thus, let the past rest where shadows play,
It has spoken, it's had its say,
Unfix the gaze from the rearview mirror,
Ahead lies the path, and it's drawing nearer.

For the past is just that for a reason,
A lesson learned, a seasoned season,
Let go the reins of what cannot be fixed,
Stride forth unchained, in the now be mixed.

12. Seeking Serenity

Tread softly through the clamor and the rush,
Recall the tranquil solace found in hush.
As much as can be done without conceding,
Strive to maintain a peace with all, unyielding.

Express your own deep truth with gentle words;
And hearken to those thought to have less worth.
All voices, though perhaps perceived as weak,
Hold tales that wait for their turn to speak.

Shun those whose presence breeds a troubled breath;
Their energies negate the soul's wealth.
If measuring yourself against another,
Fosters in you spite, then step back further.

Cherish your triumphs and the paths you plot.
Value your vocation, though it may seem slight;
It holds continuity in turbulent times,
A steadfast anchor as the tides climb.

In dealings, lead with prudence and with care,
For deceit lies masked as fair.
Still, let not suspicion veil the good
Where high pursuits are understood.

Remain authentic to your core,
Feign not warmth if it's not sure.
Hold not a jaded heart on love,
For its returns are manifold above.

Accept the wisdom aging years bestow,
Releasing youthful frolics slow.
Build resilience, for life's unseen blows;
Eschew the shadows of imagined foes.

Adopt kind discipline as lifelong pace,
But with compassion grant yourself grace.
You belong within this vast design,
No less than stars and trees align.

Though clarity might not the paths reveal,
Trust the cosmos spins with purpose real.
Find peace with the Divine, embrace
Your endeavors and the quest for inner grace.

In life's perpetual disarray, preserve
A calm within your soul, unswerved.

Despite the world's facade and ache,
It's beauty—relent, rejoice, partake.
Seek joy amidst the flux, aspire to light—
For even now, the world remains a sight.

13. Triumph Over Trepidation

In the shadow of doubt, defeat may lie,
Should you whisper to yourself, "Why even try?"
When the heart yearns to win, yet fears it may fail,
Such timid thoughts will tip the scale.

The loss is sealed when given in to fear,
In this vast world, this much is clear:
Victory starts in the will's quiet place,
Where thoughts shape the mind, the heart, the race.

Feel outclassed? Then defeated you may stand,
Yet, aim for the stars, and you'll command
Yourself to rise, to own the fight,
Before the prize shines bright in sight.

Not always to the swift or strong, do the spoils belong,
Often it's he who in the darkest times stayed resolute
and long
Who at last breaks the tape, who overcomes,

It's the steadfast soul who thinks he can and wins the
sum.

21

14. A Dance with Oblivion

Beside the whispering stream, I wandered deep in
thought,
On the crumbling verge I lingered, where reflections
fought.
My mind, a barren vessel, could not its troubles sort,
Thus, into the depths I plunged, where solace sought.

Thrice I broke the surface, gasping for the air,
Thrice the chill of water proclaimed its biting flair.
Had the stream not grasped me with its icy dare,
My breath would now be mingled with the cold abyss's
glare.

Yet, oh how chilly was the stream! How bitterly it stung!

Upon the roof I wandered, high above the roar,
Images of love lost in my mind did soar.
Poised upon that precipice, I faced the tempting door,
A leap towards oblivion, from heartache to ignore.

There I stood and wailed against the void profound,
There my tears bore witness, to the depths unbound.
If not for the dizzying heights that kept me sound,
I might have fallen freely, to where peace is found.

Oh, how dizzy were those heights! How fearfully
profound!

Yet here I stand among the living, though oft it seems a
chore,
Not yet destined to depart through that shadowed door.
I've danced with stark oblivion, felt its cold, hard floor,
Yet in this life's embrace, I find worth fighting for.

Hear me should I bellow, see me should I weep,
This soul of mine is rugged; its climb is long and steep.
Mark me not as vanquished—I have promises to keep,
For death will have to tarry, however my heart may leap.

Oh, life pulses on—rich as aged wine, bold and deep!

15. When the Night Falls

Who shapes the curve of the stream?
Who paints the dusk and the dawn?
Who designs the dance of the leaf?
This leaf, I speak of—
the one that pirouettes from the mighty oak,
the one that whispers secrets to the wind,
who twirls through air, not merely falling down—
who can catch the eye with its graceful descent.
Now it settles soft upon the fertile earth,
Now it cradles dew, and quietly decays.

I am not certain what dreams may come.
I do see how to watch, how to truly see,
to lie amidst the shadows on the ground,
to embrace the soil beneath the sky,
how to roam with a quiet heart through reveled peace,
which has cradled me in reflective hours.
Was there more to do, beneath the sun's ardent gaze?
Does not all drift softly towards gentle night?

Consider, as the sun fades into the enveloping shade—
What mark will you leave on the enduring Earth?

25

16. Dusk to Dawn

Then came the moment, profound and so clear,
To embrace life wholly, I must let go the fear.
In seeking the vigor of life's full embrace,
My doubts and my terrors needed to erase.

So with a deep breath, I chose to defy,
The shadows that haunted, from my mind they'd fly.
Releasing the fright that constrained my soul's flight,
I found my full self in the brave, bold daylight.

No longer encaged by my old timid ways,
I stepped into sunlight, and savored its rays.
Once fear was forsaken, and courage took hold,
My life grew in stories that begged to be told.

17. I am who I am

In this fleeting life, I seek a rapid trail,
Laughter echoes as time does sail.
Death may lurk, a whisper close,
Echoed by voices, harsh and morose.

I scorn the hate that words can weave,
Being myself is my reprieve.
Speak if you will, there's no contest here,
Friendship blossoms from those sincere.

If disdain is all you choose to share,
Save your breath, I shall not care.
Unliked by some who judge so strict,
Yet love prevails, it's love I pick.

No need for handshakes or empty stares,
Your discomfort is yours alone to bear.
What you see, if it displeases, leave,
In my essence, I believe.

I stand firm, I am who I am,
Understanding is a bridge, not a dam.
And if understanding is too grand a plan,
Remember, it matters not, in the vast life's span.

18. Never to Fall

Witness my trials, yet watch me stand,
No fall from grace, no dropped hand.
For strength prevails where weakness calls,
I rise above the deepest falls.

The world proclaims, "The path is clear,"
Yet walking it whispers fear.
Obstacles dressed in daily disguise,
A test of will before dawn's rise.

Hardships mount, a daunting lot,
Life's forge heats, my resolve taut.
Behind my smile, a tear might lurk,
Braving each day - that's the real work.

In battles fought, a silent plea,
To live despite mortality.
Through tempests tough, I may stagger small,
You'll see me bend, but never sprawl.

So mark these words, my solemn vow,
Through storm and trial, I won't bow.
For life's cruel game plays fierce and tall,
You'll see me strive—never to fall.

19. Unleash

In shadows of fear and confusion,
Do you feel your hopes are mere illusion?
Yet, unwritten are the finest tales,
Unrun are the most transformative trails.

The unrivaled goal remains unmet,
Unsung is the finest quartet,
Melodies await their sweetest set—
Rise up, the dawn is fresh and wet!

The globe, in earnest need, calls loud
For your craft, to pierce the common shroud.
Its treasures of joy are yet lean,
Cries for beauty it has not seen.

Thirsts for strength, desires more dance,
For passion, truth, and high romance.
Commitment, zeal—this is your stance,
In chance's garden, take your chance!

For words of depth are still to rhyme,
Dream homes await their design sublime.
The loftiest summits yearn your climb,
Vast rivers seek new bridges in time.

Banish your doubts, brave heart, proceed,
The seeds of greatness start as seed.
For jobs supreme are yet to heed,
The finest deeds are yours to lead.

20. Never Alone

As you venture through life's vast expanse,
With winding paths that twist and dance,
The truest essence you shall pursue
Is the authentic self, forever true.

Hold firm to who you are within,
Through testing times and trials grim.
Cling tightly to your dreams so vast,
For in their pursuit, your life is cast.

Encounter you will, falter and defeat,
And bitter tastes that none would seek,
Yet rise above each trying bout,
For in your strength, your soul speaks out.

Amidst life's rush, pause to smile,
Savor moments, rest awhile.
Carve your memories with gentle care,
For joy resides in moments shared.

As your voyage unwinds, day by day,
Remember, you're not lone on this fray.
My heart, a beacon steadfast and true,
A home awaits in comfort for you.

21. Life's Tapestry

May you find within life's ebb and flow
Enough joy to soften deepest woe,
Enough challenge to forge your strength,
And sorrow's touch, to temper at length.

May hope be the lamp that lights your way,
Its glow warming each and every day,
With failures that teach humility's grace,
And triumphs that quicken your soul's pace.

Surrounded by friends who share and care,
Wealth enough to sustain and spare,
An eager spirit that never rests,
Pushing forward to meet new quests.

With resolve firm, unwavering, true,
Strive to make each day anew,
Better than the last, a rising sun,
In the endless quest, till life is done.